Books by Cynthia Macdonald

I CAN'T REMEMBER

CYNTHIA MACDONALD

POEMS
I CAN'T REMEMBER

Alfred A. Knopf   New York   1997

Copyright © 1997 by Cynthia Macdonald

All rights reserved under International and Pan-American Copyright Conventions. Published in the United States by Alfred A. Knopf, Inc., New York, and simultaneously in Canada by Random House of Canada Limited, Toronto. Distributed by Random House, Inc., New York.

http://www.randomhouse.com/

Acknowledgment is made to the following publications in which some of the poems in this book first appeared:
Antaeus: "Children Who Fall Off the Edge of the World Because of Secrets"
The New Yorker: "Divining Rod"
The Paris Review: "The Dreamer on the Stone Couch Dreams and Wakes"
Prairie Schooner: "Casual Neglects," "Miriam's Grandmother," "Singing Miriam's Lament," "Maps and Globes," "Vermeer's Lady Reading at an Open Window," "Jesus Returns"
TriQuarterly 95: "How William Solomon Invoked Free Will," "The Great 14th Street Costume Company"
"Mary Cassatt's Ten Hours in the Pleasure Quarter" was written for and was published in *Transforming Visions: Writers on Art,* edited by Edward Hirsch.

Thanks to the Folger Shakespeare Library for awarding me the O.B. Hardison Poetry Prize; the honor made me happy; the monies attached enabled me to take time off to write some of the poems in this volume.

Manufactured in the United States of America
First Edition

FOR JIM — FIVE SPECIAL YEARS TO REMEMBER

Invent the truth.   *Giuseppe Verdi*

Maybe I found something that day
that had been lost.
Maybe I lost something that turned up later.
            Wislawa Szymborska

CONTENTS

I

I I

I

CHILDREN WHO FALL OFF THE EDGE OF THE WORLD BECAUSE OF SECRETS

I

Cloves. Like the nipples of a child emerging from the falls'
cold water in the Moluccas. Spice: embedded in the Indonesian
Archipelago. Cloves stuck in Easter ham, remnant of that time
when cloves preserved the meat from iridescent spoils.

Spice routes. Sought and fought for. Through the dark continent—
its pungent wetnesses, its dry and curving inland seas—Spain,
Portugal, the Netherlands and France searched for routes;
they probed the oceans past yellow-streaked Canary Isles,
past bronze-green silk Cape Verde Islands and round
the Atlantic curve of land which would become the Ivory Coast.

Searching for the passage, bumping once and twice and then
times beyond count into the coast (like children's sailboats, rudder set,
bumping against the stone rim of the park's calm sailing pond),
hoping to find a shining water pathway to the studded isles.
In 1499 da Gama did. It took two years, three months
from Lisbon round Good Hope to Calicut and the Spice Islands.

II

The Portuguese, who'd banked on being first and were,
knew that the secret must be kept. The sailors pledged to secrecy
on pain of death—and it was painful, long and full of suffering
to make example of the fate of slippery tongues—did learn to
hold them. But still, there was the question of the maps and charts.
How to create and store them, keep them safe from foreign bribes?

The answer: children who'd just been taught to read and write.
Not old enough to understand the import of the whole.
Yet even so each child was given only a small part to copy
from a slivered portion of a map. And then moved to the next.
A fifteenth century assembly line. No way
that she or he could possibly make sense out of the whole.
As children never can. We try to put the map together,
placing pink with pink, assessing a small sweep of curve
to find a match, puzzling over *Mada* to see if
land or *nesia* or *gascar* will fit and tell us what we
need to know to let us know the edge of love is close.

III

A mother writes from Lisbon to her older sister in 1499:
"Our dear Luiz, just six, came home this day. We did not know
he'd smuggled out the quill with which he wrote upon the maps.
Into the olive grove, he went with it; I know not why.
We found him there much later already stiffening.
He'd got the point part of the pen cross-throat. I catched him in
my arms and put my fingers down. Of course, it was too late.

And this after tansy, sotherwood and cloves mixed in with Port
had kept him from the plague. We do not know what means to take . . .
His delicate favour and bright amber eye was so deep
imprinted in our hearts, far to surpass our grief for the decease
of his three elder brothers who, dying soon as they were
born, were not so sweet endeared to us as this one was.
God grant that he may find safe harbour and a trusty map of heaven
to bring him to the laps of angels. God grant us sorrow's peace."

WHAT HEAT SIGNIFIES

Thank God, cold weather finally here—November,
10 AM, 45 degrees. (Last week, 88.) Sky, polyester bright
blue. Daytime white moon, a condom just beginning to
be unrolled, like those I made into dolls' caps after
I'd uncovered them in Daddy's bedside table. The gold-dressed
Emperor and his wife Kumiko had to pull them off because
they were so tight they brought on headache. That was in L. A.
with its boring weather, boring into me and my mother,
who fled back East, pulling me behind like a dinghy in a riptide.
I didn't know why. Only later: Daddy had been slipping
his slick, rubber-bound prick into too many others.
It was good to get back to the sharp New York winters.

For someone always ripped away, feeling bleaches out
like laundry, white and cool as a daytime moon.
For someone always ripped away, not only me
but you, Kate, whose father, hit by Zero fire, died
before you were born; so you were torn away by arms
from his when he no longer had them. And you, Faith,
whose husband left for his rival's wife, though that wife—
Mother—was abandoned in the house called *Mon Repos* where
she had wrapped him in her long black hair and April in Paris
Eau de Toilette. And for the inventor of psychoanalysis
whose nursemaid, more mother than his mother, was fired
because they said she stole his toys. So Sigi tried to steal
into the cupboard, that jail they said she had been sent to,
to steal her back, to cradle her in his arms,
to keep her safe; but she was gone.

For those who have been ripped away, there can never be safety.
We always recognize each other by our clothes,
the bleached laces and linens, the tropic cottons, the whitest shirts,
our very skin, which signifies, like a white moon,
what we have ritualized, the *Kabuki* of our confusion.

My father died. Heart failure. My father by choice.
Choice father. And a tree fell on my parked car.
The tree could have caused any death, any
destruction. It could have been a child, the intolerable
lick-luck, fate, Chinese puzzles, inscrutability,
intolerable pain. Inscrutable, racist, a canard—
Peking Duck. Yes, let's eat. First the skin
baked into translucency, the remnant fat smearing,
closing over. Then the flesh, elusive in its reminders,
its slow, reflexive pleasures. Then broth made from
what is left. Funeral meats, East and West.

Jingle words like coins, the change, or covering
for dead eyes. Fingers fiddle. Don't pick.
How many times have I told you not to?
Don't pick. But can choose. Cannot choose
the first father, the birth father who killed himself.
Did not choose the second, even prayed.
Cannot choose which death. It could have been a child.
Heads, tails. The owner-chef stands at our table, cleaver
in hand, dicing everything, showering parts into the wok,
showing off his skill. Good luck will come

in the year of the monkey. Seven come eleven.
Three men can keep a secret if two of them are dead.
Yes, but the secret is only safe when all three are.
They are. Check the car. Though dented it starts.
Both children answer the phone. We will be
home soon. But words cleave, uncertain,

7

disconsolate. They are severed but cling together.
As the children will when they go to bed;
they know he is dead. There is too much
we cannot outwit. The check, please. Have
a sugared walnut. It could have been my child.

WHAT NO ONE SHOULD WANT TO HAVE

Prague 1983

Now they are behind bars
they can say what they could
never find the means to say before
because here in prison
they are not allowed to say it.

Their eyes cast down—remembering
a father and his boy being taken away,
a singer not allowed to sing—
become eyes cast down to pray,
or to net what is beneath

the water's blue scales, such
beautiful music, the stone music
of the street where stone yields
the language everyone
understands but no one speaks.

There are statues celebrating
family life: stone mothers holding
babies, stirring pots, stone fathers
tossing balls to sons, stone lovers
reading *Il Paradiso,* releasing

their tears only in the rain
where, above all—stone yielding
the language everyone understands
but cannot speak—poets carve what
they are not allowed to say.

9

But we . . . we search
the dump for bones
hoping to find something
besides our own flesh
to sink our teeth into.

THE DREAMER ON THE STONE COUCH DREAMS AND WAKES

1. *The Young Woman Who Lies in a Shoe*

A woman of wool lies on a couch covered with pale shawls.
The way it holds her, she and the couch are almost one.
Cold fingers the shawls but she is warm. Though gravely ill.
Her family is wreathed around her. She lies in the living room
Of their shoe, which will soon become the dying room.

To her mother who remembers how they laid them out
In the old country, the coffee table beside the couch is a board
Where they will turn her daughter in a winding sheet;
To her husband, the table is a coffin; to her children,
A headstone, much like the headboard of the bed she no longer
Inhabits because she wishes to be with them to the last.
And to her baby girl, the table is a place different from
The hilly warmth of mother. It is evening: clear twilight.
Her husband remembers spring nights when they first met,
How they knit together and never raveled.
The woman breathes her last—the baby atop her—
And her flesh begins to harden, wool to wood.

2. *The Young Woman Who Dies in a Shoe*

A woman lies on a couch, plumped pillows behind
Her head. Lies come from her mouth like time
Lapse films of a tree bursting into leaf—
That she is not in pain, that she will not die.
Her baby crawls out of her, pushed out by

A growth, her second swelling in nine months.
The family gathers around her, crying. She has
Small elegant feet, one clad in a fine green shoe.

3.   *The Man Whose Young Wife Died*

The man is lying on a stone couch—the sidewalk where it meets
The church's wall. He is trying to feed discarded chicken skin
To the baby who cannot eat. In his pocket the green shoe;
Its high heel causes him pain, which reminds him of the unhealed
Wound of Amfortas, reminds him of how the baby in his arms
Entered the world. He hums a phrase of Parsifal
As if it were food snagged from the trash can.
The other children have been disposed of by agencies.
He should take the baby to Bellevue. He will
As soon as his wool wife comes home to lie with him.

WHAT IS NEVER LOST

Well, each of us is prone to disarray.
I am always set for a disaster
knowing one will come, and it will stay

until it has destroyed me in some way.
I save gold ribbons, purple alabasters;
well, each of us is prone to disarray.

And then there are the plagues to keep at bay
by stocking Gatorade and mustard plasters.
I'm sure the plague will come and it will stay

and all the ones I love will pass away
or come too close and make me a Jocasta.
Well, each of us is prone to disarray.

The stock market will crash—perhaps today
so I can't go when you go to Alaska.
The breadline's soon to come and it will stay.

I pile up, ward off, eat down to allay
the fears of death and loss I cannot master.
Well, each of us is prone to disarray
not knowing when and where and who will stay.

THE BLUE BOY AND THE PINK LADY

He was all in shimmering satin when first I saw him
on a playing card. We traded them in 1948,
value based on eight-year-old aesthetic judgment. He stood
against a storm-lit scene of hills and trees and flashy glowering
sky, holding a white plumed hat. Handsome but not a man,
more like a Disney prince than Cornell Wilde who'd later won
his way into my heart by coughing so much blood as Chopin.
Merle Oberon as George Sand was something else.
I wondered if I'd like to be like her and thought
I wouldn't: those cigars. Blue Boy had only me until

May Cohen brought Pink Lady to the park one day.
Yes, they were perfect, she wafting her filmy gown
of white, her sash and satin bonnet, rosy pink
to match her lips and cheeks. The sky behind was
azure swirled with clouds. I put them side-by-side
until the fingered edges of the cards turned grey.
In storage—1986—my mother, ten years dead, woke up
as daughter Jennifer and I went through the boxes
and the hanging wardrobes of her things. We felt her there.
The warehouse on that bleak November day was 52 degrees.

We worked in winter coats and heavy gloves
and still were chilled. Yet even in the cold, Dorothy
Kiam Lee Hirst—Mummy or Tanny—was there
in every chair and chest and on the grass-green loveseat.
Jennifer held up two heavy maroon volumes, "Look."
We put them on the spoiled dining-room table—
there'd been a leak—*Famous Paintings*—and, in gold,

Miss Dorothy Kiam. Inside, between the flyleaf and
page one, were The Blue Boy (Master Jonathan Buttall).
Gainsborough. And Pinkie (Miss Sarah Moulton-Barrett).
Sir Thomas Lawrence. Buttall. Buttall. That couldn't be

his name, my sweet blue satin boy. But then, how could
the prince and princess get divorced? They did
a few months after Mummy took me to the big museum
where—surprise—Pinkie and Blue Boy hung.
"You may buy any print you want to for your room."
"May I buy two?" They went with me and then had
disappeared only to be found again after another death.
Daddy's mother's silver is all mixed up with
Mummy's grandmother's. When last I saw him
in shimmering L.A., the prince was all in grey and rue.
And "things will never be the same again" was true.

CASUAL NEGLECTS

People forget their children in the strangest places.
Crossing Fifth in front of Saks, Little Jane
left behind. In the basket of a bicycle, then out of it,
Little Paul whose absence was unnoticed until
a neighbor brought him home. Little Raylinn of the
Projects left at Burger King while Mama met
her mark in Union City. And Little Hetty home from
school to find an empty house cleared of its furniture.
Her Mom forgot to tell her they were moving.

And then there's What's-Its Name who watches over us,
checking his wrist to see if the time is right, patting
her breast to check the milk run, folding the timetable,
pulling its trunk with its trunk when it moves toward
India. The celestial throne is passing hard and the studded
jewels poke What's-At-The-Bottom of it all. We prod
the godly cheek so It/She/He, He/It/She slides off; the left
behind, to be exact: that's us. The air is absent-minded
and the empty sky of Paradise is pocked with small pink shells,
those baby fingernails which couldn't quite keep holding on.

HOWARD TAKES THE FIFTH

in memory of Howard Moss

Howard: today I saw you going into the Fifth Avenue
Cleaner ($1.95 For Any Garment) on Bissonnet in Houston.
How perfect for you, an absolute New Yorker, to go to Fifth,
The element which the Pythagoreans added to air, fire,
Water, earth—that fifth of which the heavenly bodies

Were composed. As you composed *Beach Glass* and *Stars*
And read them over lunch at One Fifth Avenue; they were
An obbligato to the meal. Parallel fifths so common
In Middle Ages plain chant, but banned in later harmony
The oxtail soup was specially delicious on the winter day.

Stopped on Bissonnet, I see your back, the camel hair sweater
You often wore, a bit more stooped than when I saw you last,
But looking fit. The Cleaner wasn't here on that visit
The year you died. Along the curb are bits of clear and red glass,
Asphalt beach glass. The light turns green as you turn back—

Something forgotten in the car you only learned to drive when
You were fifty—and so I glimpse your face before the traffic
Drives me on. And it is you. Your smile gives you away,
That thin, wavy line as if drawn by a nursery child or someone
With late Parkinsons. I wave at you; you do not see.

This city is where you were before you went back to
New York to die. Of course, it can't be you on Bissonnet.
The flowers on your grandma's headstone turned to moss.
And yours? Are you up there reposing on celestial furniture,
Stars in your eyes? Houdini failed to answer, but I'll ask anyway.

"Dear Mr. Moss, This is a true poem for you. Please let me
Know if there is hope and tell me what you think asap."
Some day we hope to meet you, Someday, we know not when,
We shall meet in a better land, And never part again.
Lovingly remembered by your friends. "Enclosed an sase."

I tell myself once more it is not you in Houston. But there is singing
And there are stars in the blue banner of Texas sky where I want
to write *I Miss You.* The Cleaners' sign is neon, white and red;
I wish I could believe that all celestial furniture was strewn
for comfort up in heaven, Howard, where if it is, you are.

JESUS RETURNS

I am Jesus.
No, I do not think I am. I am. Believe me.
If I must, I will perform miracles for you.
But I never liked that aspect of my earthly visitation—
a bit hokey, don't you agree? I had hoped this time
to do without multiplying the red bream and the loaves.
Perhaps I can. The older broom of earth
sweeping around the sun will tell.
Housekeeping—that's why I'm here. My Father
could not seem to get it right without

my personal appearance. You genuflect?
Have you forgotten I was Jewish?
That made my heavenly Father Jewish,
Mary and Joseph, too. As Jewishness descends
through the maternal line, it means we all are.
The way I argue this is so Talmudic, it proves the point.
Unless when I was Christianized I was a Jesuit.
And then there are the Buddhists whose arguments
are unopposed. One hand makes manifold
the lack of opposition. If you believe me—

I see by your eyes you do—then welcome me:
Christ in my bed on earth again and not a single scar.
The only nails are on my fingers and toes.
Balm of balsam, that's what did it, and juice
of the white heal-all. You still don't seem to understand
however clearly I explain that in the land I visited,
just after B.C. ended, the local populace was Jewish.

Only the intruders, Egyptians from the land of Ptha
and Romans full of Jupiter and Mars, were scattered
through the Judaic mosaic. To keep the tile agleam

use pomegranates sieved of seeds mixed with Mr. Clean.
It's pleasant here in Amarillo, reminds me some of Bethlehem.
Do you imagine Paradise is interesting? Eternal bliss?
How do you think of it? Such bliss as may be had is where
you are. Where we are now. That is my message.
Perhaps that is my message. The time of certainty is past.
Certainty is today's poison. I have to stick the meat thermometer
into the chicken and baste it every fifteen minutes.
Of that I'm certain. You think the way I speak is not poetic,

no sweeping phrases? Remember I must use the language of today.
What can I do to move the world into the paths of generosity
and kindness? How can I know? But I must try. A vision: my
father is pulling hairs out of his head. The skin he frees of hair
will be a halo for the century to be. And all of you who were so
full of certainty about my second coming will be confused and
certainly dismayed. Too bad. I have to go and mop the floor of
Bosnia. I have to trellis and then train the *Star of Bethlehem*
to meet itself. I have to sweep the sky of the spilt milky way.

Dark night ahead.

I I

A murdered chicken will be served.   *Mary Shelley*

CHICKEN LITTLE

The reason he ran around
was because his brother died
and the sky was really falling down.

The reason she ran around
was because the old smut man
was chasing her and she could not
find a safe house. And the sky fell.

The reason they ran around
was they were not allowed
to sleep in the park.
They saw the cruel, cold
sky wheel and fall.

The reason we all run around
is that we see but cannot change what
we see: the church stairs ice,
big chunks of red crash down
from the broken bowl of the sky,
snow feathers clump into white wings.

WHO IS CHICKEN?

Silver Duckwing game
cock dares his son to fight him.
Chicken agrees and puts on
silver spurs, made for him by
silversmiths in Cockspur Street;
his father's are of gold.
The barnyard pit is lined
with spectators wearing
feather cloaks of many colors.
Chicken feels acid swirling in
the pit of his stomach and knots
in his spine. Not because he will
lose, but because he will win.
The king has to prove he is
a young cock by risking more
than he ever risked when young.
And Chicken is snared in a trap
which he can escape only by
slashing thrusts of murder.

CHICKEN SLIPPERS

The chicken's beak had pecked her sister's eyes—Christina's eyes
blank blue and dead—and so they had to close them when she died.

The Doctor came to tell her she had died. He sat her on his lap and said,
"sit here, Diane, I've got to tell you something very sad.

Christina died today." "Oh. Did it hurt?" And Di began to cry.
She knew that Doctor Jones thought she was sad; that wasn't why.

It was because the chicken slippers were so mad and cross
as if they were Christina's eyes behind her gold-rimmed glasses.

And at the church where smells of funeral were in the air,
she, still alive, was not allowed to go; that was unfair,

and even all the Easter flowers could not hide the stink
of bad, bad chickens. When she asked Dr. Jones—no tears, just blinks—

if it had hurt, he told her that Christina shut her dead blue eyes
and went to sleep looking at the Easter Baskets full of lilies.

"Were there chickens in them?" she asked. "No, there might
have been a bunny." She jumped down off his lap. Pure white

lilies filled with egg-yolk yellow chicks; she knew
that's what Christina had seen. "Not even just a few?"

She turned. "Just a few, a few?" she said to Dr. Jones.
"Diane, she's up in heaven now, playing." "Her bones,

maybe she stuffed the chickens in her bones." He looked at her.
He did not know about those chicken slippers, so furry

and so warm. And how she'd tried to put the slippers on
and yelled at Tina, stuck out her tongue and swore

when Tina said, "They're mine; you can't." That was the last
time she ever saw her sister. She's forty now and all of that is past.

She tells about the soft, warm bunny she gave Tina just before
she died and often orders lots of deep-fried chicken: extra crispy.

ONCE YOU NOTICE CHICKENS THEY ARE EVERYWHERE

In the Brazos Bookstore Children's Section:
Chickens! Chickens! and *The Painter who Loved Chickens.*

In the Museum: Hokusai's woodblock print:
Rooster and Hens, and Goya's etchings of chicken whores.

Under glass: Alice B. Toklas's:
Chicken In Half Mourning with Madeira and Truffles.

Chickens become Hungarians, not as Paprikash, but as everywhere—
even when you don't want to have the Magyar infection,

the fever that you suffered for two years
after tall, blond, married Margareta stole

your lover who left you in a boarding house in Pesth
to be with her and cursed because you would not

keep his luggage while he looked and found
a hotel for their love nest. It was the Hilton.

The kitchen garden of the boarding house had six hens
that clucked and seemed to shake their feathers in dismay,

but at that time—so long ago—you hardly noticed chickens.
"If you have Hungarians for friends you do not need an enemy,"

the saying goes. From *The Complete Poems of Miklós Radnóti:*
"Thick woods surround me; in a dust cloud the far-off flock."

ROOSTER PETER

Think of all those waiting
for his chickens to come home to
roost. Two wives, and his current
one, and his many children,
hatched with rooster indifference
to hatching. O, what a lovely cockscomb
shining translucent red in the rising
backyard sun! And surely
there are others, hurt not by attack—
though he has had many a cockfight

and won; those do not count;
rivals would have clawed out
his eyes with their scalpel claws
if he hadn't struck first—but hurt
by a casual turning of the head.
Away. As if they were nothing.
As if he were alone, his thoughts
like downy feathers blowing
where the wind lofts them.
You may be sure

his chickens are coming home
filled with what he has taught them.
He stands in the vermilion light
of sunset, feathers dusty with age.
His chickens have arrived.

They cluster together in
the red wheelbarrow, pecking
at rain-glazed wood, waiting
for when he will need them,
for when they can refuse him.

CHICKEN PARTS

from his beloved wife—he always calls her that—
whistling "Bang, Bang, Maxwell's Silverhammer"
as he struts the streets of Chicago. This used to be
where the stockyards were. No hog butchers,
no fog, no cats today. He gets on the train
at the loop going to his job at the parts
factory. His stop. He gets off on
thinking of his beloved's feather ruff. The bust
of Frank Perdue stares down at him from above.
Punch the time clock. Judy, his sweetie, will be
ready to peck him when he gets home. She is angry
that he stops at his bar on the way. Sunset
and evening star and one clear crow for a beer.
Well, more than one. He moves to his station on
the line. It's all her fault. The bell rings, the line
begins to move. He eviscerates each body
and throws it in the disinfecting bath, whistling
"Bang, Bang, Maxwell's Silverhammer came down
on her head." Early in his job he used to notice
any body might be a relative, a second cousin
once removed, someone like that. The line moves
in a circle. Bang, Bang. Cold steam rises from
the vat beside him. His headaches punctuate the day.

POET-CHICKEN ANSWERS THE INTERVIEWER

There is only one thing you may not ask me. And you know
what it is. That is the boundary I will not cross.
The foxes wait outside.

I don't give a flying fuck how many want to know why
we cross the road. They'll find out or they won't.
Would you like some corn bread?

My working methods are to sit on my tail till inspiration,
that horsefly, bites. Then if I can, to throw the buzz away
and keep the path of flight.

Of course I think of form. I am a Southerner. Formality
and courtesy are how we've kept on going. And coarseness
rough as homespun.

No. No computer. There are so many turkey quills about.
Ben Franklin wrote Poor Richard's Almanac standing.
I'm somewhat shaped like him, and do the same.

I count the pebbles in my crop to find the accented words.
Some are bright as tourmalines or deep as topaz.
But that is rare.

Let others cluck. I use the language of the barnyard only
when it must be used. But I would sooner pluck
delight from air. Or airs. That is as songs but not

as false elaboration. The argument between "the raw"
and "cooked" is one I will not entertain. Yes, Levi-Strauss
was correct, but the use of terms is not determined

by the one who coins them. First they're bright as silver
in the sun, then scratched and dulled like long-used
quarters. No, not the hen house.

I will not crow about myself; I'll only say perhaps
I have come close to *the beautiful circuit of thought
and desire,* as Henry James described it.

Again, the road. The other side? I said I would not answer.
Perhaps to find a pail of time? A tall, red barn?
A star? Foxes on the yellow line?

JEWISH CHICKEN EXAMINES THE DIFFERENCE
BETWEEN HEAVEN AND HELL

Chicken listens to Pastor Peter Imbrich:
So you were saved forty years ago
and you haven't been to church
since? You think you're going to Heaven?
Well, you won't—going to Heaven is
like being in church all the time.

Chicken reads: This week
is the fiftieth anniversary of Auschwitz.
The only way out was through
the crematorium chimney.

Chicken smokes and thinks. Smoke rises.
He blows rings and feels his lungs
crisping. He blows rings
seeing halos. He smells barbecue
from next door: family burning.

LIKE A CHICKEN

I tell you—
she speaks through her neck.
She runs around and around
like a chicken with her head cut off.
She is a chicken with her head cut off.

Threads of memory remain—
I wonder why—but she cannot
depend on them. Always trying
to grasp what she is severed from.

Loss is the greatest fear, a pendant
hanging from the cut just below
the head's severing point. She's trying
to remember the name of that Queen,

the one with six fingers who had
her sleeves cut long to hide deformity,
the one who also lost her head.
I know it's Anne Boleyn, and once

she might have. But she does not.
She hears the lute, its music
sweet as love once was.
Good night, sweet head, goodnight.

RETRIEVAL

A *Silver Duckwing* Gamecock,
a *Cochin China* fowl,
a *Crowned Langshan* pullet,
      the date that Aunt Joe died,
   a *Snowshoe* hare,
a *Chittergong* hen,
      my New York dentist's name,
a *Frizzle* hen,
   an *Eastern Cottontail,*
an *Aseel Indian* cock,
a spangled *Silver Moonie* chick,
      that poem about rapture,
   a *Blacktailed* Jackrabbit,
a *Crève-Coeur* rooster.
      I am trying to remember.

SPEARVILLE, KANSAS

There were lots of chickens on the farm,
but this one was his pet. He named it
Clarence for that dead big brother
who'd been killed: his arm caught in
the threshing machine. Clarence, *a Barred
Plymouth Rock,* went everywhere with him.

That day in the ripe berry patch, the patch
where he'd been sent to pick worms off
the fruit, Clarence was beside him, walking
the rows of red Valentine heart berries,
berries you'd have thought Clarence might
have pecked at, but he never did.

So the boy dropped the choicest worms
into Clarence's mouth, telling him
"good chicken, best chicken." And his beak
opened almost as if he were a mechanical
marvel. A marvel until he died. Too much
fulfillment can kill you. When the boy

grew up he became a famous surgeon.
The intestinal tract. Sunday: Bible study.
Two of his sons, Billy and Robert,
were born with big strawberry marks
on their faces. But that is surely just
coincidence, surely not just punishment.

III

HOW WILLIAM SOLOMON INVOKES FREE WILL

It's all over. It didn't work. Will never work. All water
under the dam. Because, you see, what you said you wanted
and what I thought you said you wanted were not the same.
Our overalls were: typical blue denim,
good for the work at hand. But I couldn't get
the wheelbarrow to wheel, which should have been
an omen—everything to do with circularity is.
There must have been a fault in the geometry
or in the earth's foundation. Even a fault corrected
changes the geography, affects cement.
There is something subversive in the wheel's fixation.
Something too intransigent. But you, singing among
the vivid greens of tropical plants, voracious orchids,
genital-pink flowers, your luna moth sleeves, your long
hair flowing, had easily turned away once it happened.

Correction: once you told me it had happened.
I, fixed on circuitry, was watching for
the first cracks to appear. It was too late
to fix them, the whole would certainly give way.
I felt a little thrill of pleasure contemplating
what would be immersed. But did not wish
to drown, myself. So, I began my solitary building,
hoping there was time before the flood. There was.
Diluted salty seas stretch out. The tides are weakened
although the sheets are often full of wind: free will.
Small wrinkles on the water break monotony:
I sail, communing with myself and God, and wonder if

there is a difference. The sky is no longer the limit.
Water is. What surfaces from down below, the stains,
the spoils, are messages from them, from you, to me.

Oh yes, I see your hair as I look down at Hammondsville.
You're pushing a shopping cart in Kroger's parking lot.
You must have returned home from that place where
false green wings pulled us apart. Home to the slush,
not quite water, not quite snow. To divide a baby
had taken all my wisdom, but it is simple to divide
a man and wife. Now you cannot undermine me,
but the whole morphology of life is changed.
What's predetermined, is. What's undermined, will.
What's overwhelmed, may be. It's all water over the bridge.
Ambiguous swallows waver, and water trickles down my throat
but never slakes my thirst. And what you said you wanted
suddenly is clear. A water desert stretches before me,
and stretches me upon the rack of perfect sky. And Will
will not be free until . . . I guess I do not know.

MARY CASSATT'S TWELVE HOURS IN
THE PLEASURE QUARTER

1 *Woman Bathing*

What is in back of the back?
Pleasure hidden behind flesh. Screened from view,
    screened as if by gold squares. Paper.
Even the mirror reflects only thin
hair, leaving excess to bloom underfoot.

2 *Utamaro's Yoshiwara District*

Silk covers the moon's face and
scenes unfold before it, a fan unfurls
    displaying reds and purples,
*Two Courtesans And A Child; Two Beauties
And A Young Man Beside A Cherry Tree.*

3 *Shared Studios*

Degas took her on. She took
him on. Imagine! This never girlish
    girl from Philadelphia.
Colors fuse, no two alike. Fingerprints.
Miss M. Cassatt announces she's at home.

4 The Country House: Seine-et-Oise

Prints streaming down, a river
of prints hung in the hall "that leads out to
   the cold glass-paned verandah
where hung the Utamaros and one or
two Hokusais," a guest's memoir recounts.

5 Retroussage: Creative Wiping

Water trickles in the cleft
of breasts. A shudder of pleasure, "How warm
   it is today." Mary wipes
the ink out of the lines, dragging ink, black
as Japanese hair. Red hair: Retroussage.

6 Daily Life

Why is she washing? To thin
The aquatint? To wash off brains laved in
   melted butter, jugged hare,
the sour milk of baby's spit-up, ink,
or paint, or juice of mutton, or semen?

7 The Great Fire

Tangerine, burnt orange, rust
ocher, orange madder: eight of the set
   of ten suffused with shades of
orange. Flame. The Pittsburgh of her birth, sky
fused to firestorms. Wet, fugitive blue.

8 *"Stop-out" Work and Burnishing*

Degas inquires, "This back, did
you draw this?" He stands in front of *Woman
Bathing.* A single stroke, a stroke
of genius, a brush with common life, a
round, around a slowly growing nipple.

9 *Gifts*

"Retrouver, retrouver," cries
Mary's parrot, Coco. Degas brings her
irises (though he hates cut
flowers) and a sonnet worked upon for
weeks: *Perroquet, á Miss Cassatt.* She smiles.

10 *Printing*

Four states for this print woman,
bathing. Inked *a la poupée* in green and light brown,
special wiping, blued copper,
the hair and leaves rebitten, darkening them.
Drypoint amidst seduction of the bath.

11 *Impressionists and Bathing*

In back of the back? Baths with
Renoir, Degas and Seurat, the pleasure
quarter. A woman's glass, face
effaced, rubbed impressions of a print, still
wet. Suffusing light the skin drinks in.

Hung on a wall, private parts
turned away, a woman by a woman
    scoops water from the moon,
her fingers twined in floating irises.
Two beauties, and a man and baby watch.

AFTERWORDS

Cassatt owned a few prints by Hokusai and a substantial number by Utamaro, including some of the series of twelve set in the pleasure quarter of Yoshiwara. It is generally agreed that this sequence of scenes from everyday life—though his prints depicted courtesans and actors—were the strongest influence on Cassatt's sequence of ten, depicting women engaged in their daily tasks and errands. The passion with which she responded to the Japanese *ukioye* is revealed in her letter to Berthe Morisot: "You could come here to dine and then we could go to see the Japanese prints at the Beaux Arts. Seriously, *you must not* miss that. For you, who wishes to make color prints, you could not dream of anything more beautiful. I already dream of it and of nothing besides color on copper. Fantin was there the 1st day I went and he was ecstatic. And Tissot was also there."

Degas and Cassatt were passionately involved with one another for many years. But no one now knows if they were lovers or if the consummation was purely artistic. Before she died, Cassatt burned his letters to her. Most of those who knew them believed that they were friends but not lovers. There was, and still is, a lot of speculation of the "did they, or didn't they" variety. In 1944 my mother, who usually got her gossip right, announced as we stood in front of a painting by Cassatt that Cassatt had remained a virgin all her life, "in spite of all those mother-holding-a-child paintings."

Mary Cassatt's Twelve Hours in the Pleasure Quarter is written in an adaptation of a Japanese form, the tanga, with the syllable count slightly expanded to allow for the differences between sentence formation in Japanese and English.

ROBERT UNDERHILL'S PRESENT

He was eight when they gave him the felt overcoat—
his birthday.

He knew it was special.

He was still reading Walter Scott not Gogol. The coat was light grey
and he was a knight in armor. It was adamant. Iced snowballs
and other missiles no longer hurt. Or barely.

He grew as do all boys who are not dwarves or midgets. The coat
grew, too. It kept pain out, and in.

He only looked at colleges in northern places.

He often drew the coat about him, like heroines
wrapping their shawls more tightly.

He was the intrepid leader through fresh snow and blue snow
and rotten ice and the Mojave.

He loved to look at women. It is difficult
to make love wearing an overcoat.

Gestalt and sandbox therapy did not help him
remove the coat, but helped him to talk about it,
to acknowledge it was there.

He knew that all the others knew, had always known.
Some urged him to undress.

He saw *La Boheme* in San Francisco and felt betrayed
when Schaunard sold his coat. Each time he played the CD
he cried at the last act.

He knew he had to get it off. Several times: Almost. Almost.
Perhaps that is exaggeration. He'd cut off a sleeve or a lapel.
But only pulled and wrenched the whole: it was so thick.

Finally, at sixty-five he knew he could not. And sank
into despair, the very state the coat was meant
to turn away.

He took a ship to France for his last meal.
He took one home to jump. Felt really pulled
him down into the deep.

MIRIAM'S GRANDMOTHER

Willi and Lotte picked raspberries each summer
to squeeze for Hinbeernsaft. A perfect pair:
Lotte could pick just high enough so Willi did not need
to stoop. Pails and pails of berries, then home
to spread them out on sheets until the kitchen surfaces
were velvet red. Then more white sheets on top
to catch the worms, the tiny green ones nestled
in the berries. They moved up toward the light,
clinging to the sheets where Willi picked them off.

The berries rested thick, ready for the press of morning
when each pink-red titty yielded up its drops of juice.
Lotte got a suck of it each time a bottle filled.
The day she went with Mama on the train to Dusseldorf
to visit Oma and Opa she carried a big bottle of juice
before her. Like a wise man in a Christmas play bearing
myrrh to the manger. Like a movie where the heroine,
running to escape the vampire, approaches the cliff edge
the audience knows is there but she does not. Her mother,

busy with the luggage and the baby, did not see but heard
the bottle crash and Lotte's cry. She stood in streams of red,
her white dress splashed with red. Red dripping
on her best white shoes. Flowers of glass, halos of glass
had formed themselves within the lake of red, and drops
of juice merged with those of blood from slivers stuck into
her legs. Tears. A small catastrophe. All their work was lost.
In grief she hit the air. Red never was the same again. In years
to come she learned much more how difficult deaths are.

It is too late to have breakfast. Blue's Cafe serves from 6 to 8 AM.
It is too late to touch you when you sleep beside me.
You are not there.
Considering my weak ankles and my middle age,
it is too late to become an Olympic-class skater.
It is too late to have lunch. Blue's Cafe serves from 12 to 3 PM
and the sushi is all gone and the halibut dried
till its bones stick out through its flesh.
It is too late to become a World War II spy, and in the next one
there will be no time to assemble spies.
It is too late to be on time for our wedding,
which, for some reason even you could not explain,
you wanted in St Patrick's Cathedral although
you are Jewish. I should have known then.
It is too late to have dinner. Blue's Cafe serves from 7 to 10 PM
and the food has become infected with toxins
so all the customers are dead in their seats.
The late Mr. and Mrs. Bixby still hold their wine glasses,
The late Mr. Porter is stiffening, his head resting in
the soup plate, which makes a halo round it.
Perhaps being on time is not always a virtue,
as Opa and Oma found out on Kristallnacht.

MAPS AND GLOBES

Greece: Ischia. Cumae. Cities on the Hellespont and Bosporus.
Al Mina: all colored Violet Red which turned to pink against
the page. We spun the conquests and alliances
with colors of our choice. My Holy Roman Empire was
Lavender. How pleasurable to stay within the lines.

And down one side we made a color key: who hated whom
and why, and then who joined them in their puffy hate—
like faces of the angry winds—to turn another country
Jungle Green or Goldenrod. Al Mina became
Antioch and changed into a lovely Silver Grey.

Each week we had the air raid drill. The Germans and
the Japanese—Spice Brown—might turn our school
and us into a smoky ruin like the ones in London where
the schools had photographs of Churchill, Roosevelt and Stalin,
chair-by-chair, comrades-in-arms. Cerulean.

Now the world is glass, a globe of glass, more fragile than
a baby's skull, and all I know is this: Haiti. Somalia. Bosnia.
It's all the same (not motive; outcome), nothing is helped
(O, maybe in the sprint, it is, but not in the long run) by war.
I would have died in Dachau or in Bergen-Belsen, had my family

not left Alsace in 1840. Ashes are used sometimes in making glass.
I think I'd fight to save my children, my city; perhaps, myself.
Red and no color: ash, sand, glass and alum tears.
Glass globe. Glass globes, joined like the body of a woman.
An hour glass. I hold it, turn it over and watch
The passionate rush of dispassionate time into my hand.

ELEGY FOR HANS

Well, Hans, today I had to throw away
the paper, pinkish-red, and white carnations
you brought from Guatemala. They have
lasted six or seven years beyond your death.
I can't remember dates when those I loved
died. Dried fruit. The florid pinks are drained of
color and the whites have greyed. Skin and hair.
You brought them in the leather suitcase where
the honey jar had leaked and filled your clothes
and my front hall floor with sticky seepage
that foiled our scrubbing. Silver barrier. The suitcase
met the curb and garbage truck; the floor incorporated
small residues. Somehow the paper flowers
wrapped in plastic were untouched. Each flower
was furled tight and had to be spread out,
petal by petal, which I did, pulling
and ruffling what seemed to be crepe paper.
Festive streamers. I put them in a cobalt blue
glass vase and took them to the entryway
to greet each visitor. O, no, you said
they need to be wavier, fuller. You sat
down on the stairs—like later passages—
and stroked each paper petal. Real flowers.
Making love. I did not want to throw them out.
The after-image of the photographs you took—
like theft—are there beside their image on
the wall. Like us. The flowers have their own
bright afterlife. Here. Right here: white paper,
Guatemala, and the fingerprints of love.

IV

"We lack information on what Bruegel's daily life was
like; thus we must depend, with some reservations, on
Bruegel's biography in Carel Van Mander's *Het Schilderboeck,*
Haarlem, 1604 . . ."

The Florentine, Ludovico Guicciardini, said
in 1567 that Pieter Bruegel was a native
of Breda. A village in the Brabant.
Van Mander thirty years later said
the village was Bruegel near Breda.
Hieronymous Cock, engraver and print merchant

"whose hand is proud and sure and vigorous"
engraved the work of Pieter Breugel.
But gave no date of birth or name of village.
In spring of 1563, Cock married
his first teacher's daughter, Mayken Coecke
who cooked her Cock such juicy dinners

that his vigour grew more proud.
But Van Mander yearned to have a village
called Breugel to justify the painter's nickname:
Breugel of the Peasants. It is asserted now
that he was city-born. In 1560 Antwerp where
he lived and worked had 78 butchers, 169 bakers,

number of candlestick makers unknown.
360 artists. This is the matter of the matter:
Big Fish Eat Little Fish, Children's Games,
The Robber of Birds' Nests, Flemish Proverbs,
Two City Dwellers Seen from the Rear, and
imagine, if you can, more artists than butchers.

LEONARDO'S ADVICE TO ARTISTS

Painting is concerned with the ten things you can see; these are: darkness and brightness, substance and color, form and place, remoteness and nearness, movement and rest.

1 *darkness and brightness*

At the fish store the walls, the tile floor,
the counters are all white. The fish are arrayed
in ranks of fillets, strips, roulades, and bodies.
And then there are the opened clams, mussels,
and oysters in their pearlescent cups,
the scallops, bay and ocean, the crabs and lobsters,
the shining squid: all bedded on translucent ice.

Mrs. Mahoney always eats fish on Friday.
Over this she still has control, unlike the Mass.
This week she asks the monger for fillet of sole;
it's really weakfish but she doesn't know.
He wraps the sole in white paper and she takes it home,
but when she opens up the fish, it has gone bad.
It lies there dark beneath her hand.

2 *substance and color*

What is often given equal weight is often not,
for example, leaving and being left,
or substance and color. Does the word 'blue' carry
the same weight as the word 'mountain'?

and then there is the problem of the choices.
'Blue Mountain' sounds like coffee
which surely appears first as smell, a sense
which has no substance.
What he chose is not what she chose.
How insubstantial: matters of the heart.

3 *form and place*

The Reform Movement of the forties took place
in New York City. But before reform was needed
there had to be form, in this case, Tammany Hall.
By then Picasso was out of his blue period
and the cracks had begun to appear,
both those verbalized and those of perspective.

He did not exactly collaborate
but was able to stay in his Paris studio
because he never stuck his neck out to help his Jewish friends,
not even Max Jacob. He could have had
his head shaved when the war ended
but he was already almost bald.
The head of the Lexington Democratic Club,
the most important reform group,
owned three Picassos. They gave
fragmented splendor to his Park Avenue apartment.

The singer has a mote in her eye
but the cascade of notes continues even though
she can barely see. Is that the castle
or Renato? She moves toward the climactic embrace,
the passionate kiss before she dies from poison,
and finds, of course, from its tremors
it is a pillar. But she continues to emote
as she slides down it to her death,
leaving the tenor to mourn her loss.

In the castle moat fish frolic
as they swim in circles
mandated by Manrico's stone design.
Man Ray's photograph sees the fish more clearly
than one can with the naked eye;
the camera's advantage, it can stop things
and keep things. Da Camera.
The high notes are thrilling. When they end
they are gone, unless . . . Da Capo.
Here comes a head bobbing along
near enough to kiss if Man Ray
could snap him to make him stay put.
Then she could pin him to her wall
like the Boy's Day carp kite
he had on his.

5 *movement and rest*

Flammable and inflammable.
When what is is and what is not is, isn't
it difficult to know if is is part
of fish or part of fission, part of pass or part of
passion. The blue
wooden flounder in the soprano's mouth
stops her from singing.
But her head splits in three, and in spite
of the pain, she sings a Schubert trio with herself.

The sea makes it clear
rest is impossible. Even when we rest
we are as hummingbirds
always in motion: flickering eyes, fluttering breaths,
emotion deepening, then welling up.
Loves and losses pounding the shore,
one wave covering another,
and another,
so what is clear is never truly clear.

VERMEER'S LADY READING AT AN OPEN WINDOW

*"The curtain in this delicate work presents a problem. Is it
in the room or in front of the picture?"*
J.M. NASH: *The Age of Rembrandt and Vermeer*

She is standing at the window.
Glints of gold, of gilt in her hair and dress—
on the crumpled paper in her hands,
on the fruit in a blue and white bowl,
on the rug covering the table—are painted
by a light more canny in its choices than
God's light through the open window.

She hangs in Dresden.
Perhaps she is a sibyl reading of the firebombing
three hundred years hence, of the light
that caused flashcars, flashparks, flashpeople
to run, burning through that German city. We read
into the event our own pain and destruction even when
it does not fit the calmness of the figure by the window.

Perhaps she holds a letter telling her her lover
has fallen picking up his sword
to fight again in Brabant's field
and will not be coming home.
Is her expression sad? It's difficult to tell.
Her gaze is steadfast but we cannot see into her eyes.
Vermeer's glints transfer transfiguration to each object.

She stands absorbed by March light.
One curtain hangs looped over the open window
whose leaded frame encases diamond panes
and those which look like tall slope-roofed houses.
The houses of the diamond cutters are still in Amsterdam
but not the Jews who lived in them. That window curtain
is inside the room. "Vermeer has a genius for evasion."

And is the other curtain—hanging from gold rings
on a rod that crosses the room
before our eyes, just where we're standing, looking—
inside the room or in front of it?
Any moment it could be drawn to keep her
safe, to keep us out. Pictures were protected by
curtains in Vermeer's time, and so were ladies.

It's difficult to give up such protections. All those
gold rings slide easily across the rod.
Abundant proof that she is married.
Or perhaps not. There is no wedding ring on her left hand.
We cannot see her right where she would wear it if
she is a Catholic. The Diet of Wurms took place
a hundred years before her reading of this letter.

All those downy peaches spilling out
of the Delft plate announce she is ripe.
Yet perhaps it is a poem she's reading,
not from a fallen lover but from herself.
That she can read is clear. In painting,
women reading books were usually Virgins being told
by haloed angels of the hallowed cargo of their bellies.

Or women reading books were almost-banished
sybils who were feared and sought.
They saw too clearly,
as if those lenses polished by Spinoza—yes,
he was Dutch—for microscopes and telescopes
were lenses in their eyes.
The woman looking down intently

is focusing the meaning of her poem.
How difficult. She cannot get
the last line right.
She wants to reach out of the frame
to pull aside the curtain so she can surely see
the clarifying light that glances off the winter road.
The last line trembles in her hands and heart.

For JANE COOPER on the occasion of her 70th birthday,
and the publication of *Green Notebook, Winter Road*

THE GREAT 14TH STREET COSTUME COMPANY
CLARENCE ERNEST KLISTER, PROP.

Portia is wearing my black velvet robe
with flap of taffeta, and red silk
cap when she enters stage left.

I consider myself King of Delight,
the Prospero of Clothing.

I am in costumes and accessories.
My father was, and deemed
his only son should follow him.
As a child I wasn't sure I was,
and would. Uncertainty for many years
is like a lilac pall or caul;
it seals you off from all you're doomed
or blessed to be. And when it's slit
you hardly know how to exist in unprotected
air. You deem the world to be too dangerous,
the only safety in the shop behind
the piles of books, or racks of costumes.

Miss Cherry Blossom, Macbeth, Martha, Hermit of Hawaii,
The Bells of Corneville, She Stoops to Conquer.

Father left me his realm.
I have not kept his silver columns
or his emerald divans. Both art and commerce—
this is both—must move along or fail.
I made a slogan to go with our name:

"We Dress The Big Productions . . .
and the Small." After all, the change
from 1870 when he was born to
1901 when I was is like the difference
between Millet and Monet.
And even though I moved the shop
uptown near R. H. Macy's,
I kept the name my father gave it.

My sister is a painter of birds. I guess
we both are steeped in plumage.
My pansy cloak of purple silk
with lilac and viola face
invokes Klimt although its lining
merges him with Munch.
It is voluminous, encompassing.
Especially when I wear the hood;
I am both hid and opened out.
Like actors. Like birds at rest
or spreading out their wings.
The flower's face, its beauty
and its grace, reminds me of my mother
who left when I was only twelve.

For boys and for the boys
they carry in them when they're grown,
the father is the brown-eyed one,
the one they can't escape
or fully understand.
You can see through eyes of blue
but not of brown. I never left Mama,
but Father . . . yes, I left him long
before he died although he never knew.
It was my secret.

Make-up: Grease Paint, Stage Powders, Liners, Cold Cream,
Burnt Cork, Mascaro, Spirit Gum.

My Uncle, though he was not really,
would give me books.
The difference between a book and theater
is that one you must enter
or it is baseless fabric,
while the other stretches out
its arms to embrace you.
My father never made his own designs,
but I did. How my name spread;
the spotlight on me: golden crown.

La Traviata, Act I. I based Violetta's gown
on Winterhalter portraits. The bodice
was dull cream-colored satin, the sleeves
finished with a double layer of gold and
cream floss fringe. Atop a foundation
of parchment Peau de Soie,
the gold organza skirt with silver paint
on its reverse would shimmer in the lights
and sequin-scatter. Like art.

Everything including undergarments, the little niceties of
dress, hair pieces, falls, wigs, bird heads, beast heads, large
human heads for sale or rental.

My Uncle brought me *Death in Venice*
so I could give a name to what I knew
I was. I was fourteen. Ariel.

*Tights, trunk-hose, bombasted breeches, petticoat
breeches; Tunics; Cross-garterings of leather, rope, or golden
thongs; Trousers of curious open work, pajama-like affairs
which Paris wore on top of Mount Ida, the Gallic ruffled
brace, the black satin of George the Third—Beau Brummel's
skin-tight trousers with slashes on the instep, Togas and all the
amplitudes, the fullest being Oxford Bags.*

Two lovers together, fit together to a T:
such a tempest, such a storm of passion.
I was King of Furbelows,
the Prospero of love and clothing.
Until forty. *Der Rosenkavalier,
Mourning Becomes Elektra, The Blue Angel.*
I am not sure exactly what
went wrong. Inevitable pratfalls?
The wear of repetition?

*Moths, and their lacy remnants, Beetles, Roaches, Rats and
other Vermin and the patterns of their droppings.*

How fortunate we are
to live with flare and fame,
with almost mastery, and never know
that they will melt into thin air:
the Himalayas are too high for breath.
I still design and have designs,
but all the gold is dark, the silver, grey,
reflecting nothing, though I do reflect.

*Mirrors to hold over mouths, pearls for the eyes, spirit
embalming stuff.*

There is a lot of life to live but seams
come to nothing. I deck myself in
Houppelandes, long all-enveloping garments
with gaily foliated sleeves that hide
what is at hand. Underneath: no scarves,
no cards, no colored flowers, no props at all.

THEIR PLACES RESOLVE AND DISSOLVE

"Illustration with attribution: Old Imari Plate: Died Brocade of a Windswept Shore"
Japanese Ceramics: *Hoikusha's Color Books Series*

I   Driving through Fields
on a summer night, the phrase translates itself to Frost's snow
even though the two are in France. And suddenly the trees fencing the fields
are rimed with ice. The light of the great moon rising is caught
in the branches' glass skin and they ignite into fiery crackling. Haloed
stars pinwheel dizzyingly. The two stop the car and get out, holding each
other for balance. The road is littered with ears—no, oyster shells.

II   Sometimes You Hear Me
but you don't hear me, the man says, as the hornless
Red-Polled cattle stand sleeping. It is almost dawn on the Imari plate
which was shipped to Sussex in 1688. Cinnebar red enamels the sky
as the sun rises; day appears, a milky blue-white glaze. Heavy rain
had fallen in the night; its wet sheet links everything as if rain were
the mind. *I do,* she says. The car's wheels throw water drops in circles.

III   Like Kenzan, the Master Potter
throwing clay. Or Koetsu's *raku* in the kiln
wheeling and cracking in the fire. The man and woman walk
the long obi of sand, strewn with seaweed, shells and beach glass,
Amagansett brocade. What's been linked once has been linked twice
by each of them: the places, the makers all seen at once, the way
the wave lapping the water overlaps itself and all that underlies it.

IV   Think of Their Heads as Jars
of dyed brocade, patterned with stars exploding
over Arles, almost funerary, for they are almost old and the door to
whatever does or does not come next on the plain of Jars is just down
the beach. *The dark is darker in winter,* she says. *Yes,* he says, taking her
hand, *don't be afraid, a door is not a door when it's ajar.* Past the door
black night floods the noon sky. *Magritte,* she says. *I will,* he says.

VICTORIA'S SECRET

The woman on the front of *Victoria's Secret* is
looking through swirls of Victorian hair—copper and gold—
at whoever is looking at her. Her purple lace body suit is holding,
but not holding up, swelling but small enough breasts.
I wish I could look like that, wearing deep purple with
sheer *point d'esprit* at my back. I think of a play

part of which is a tea where Virginia Woolf and Max Beerbohm
explore the Victorian woman of letters. They fence with
their teaspoons and tongues. Their talk is a brilliant
but quiet filigree, perhaps *point d'esprit* of sheer
desperation. Beerbohm wrote a story where a much-burnished critic
is given a book by a new woman novelist—"brilliant, it's brilliant"—

but he can't bear to read it. Thrown in his hearthfire, it somehow
won't burn. But Victoria did. She coveted Albert as if he were empire,
pressed pouty lips against his skin as if she were sealing the red wax
of state on his body. And he was embossed with roses of love bites
and, matching her passion, rose to the occasion. Yet Victorian wives
were supposed to be frigid, were told how to manage the pain

of the marriage nights: "Just grit your teeth and think of England."
The birds all wore black when old queen lady died. But they flapped
away and the flappers danced in—bobbed hair, flattened breasts and skirts
to their bottoms: my mother. Everything changed. Well, it did and it
didn't for women who write and the men who applaud them. The women
press all those Victorian remnants—dried flowers, three names—

into ivory scrapbooks and put them on shelves, up too high to reach.
"Brilliant, you are brilliant": the men repress fears as if they were
ironing and had to make sure their creases were knife-sharp.
They dream of twentieth-century Medusas of letters and call
in their sleep for the woman they love to break up the nightmare.
We waver, afraid if we soothe and amuse and mother those men,

and if we are their muses our books will be written with water,
not fire. Yet we want them to love us and lust after us.
I think of tonight, how I wish I could greet you in a body suit
purple as the iris you bring me. How I'll stand like a bride
with them in my arms as Victoria did when Albert
approached her. Or was it with violets or lilacs or larkspur?

Such royal purples. How could they unbend? But they did.
And we do. Your blue eyes are shining, your irises widen.
I see my reflection: I'm looking at you through swirls—
gold and copper—of Victorian hair that plait with
the water's cobalt and green tresses from which I'm emerging
to lie on the half-shell, Venus couchant in your arms.

DINNER BEFORE THE BLUE HORIZON

(Three born in 1928, one born in 1948)

Willard, Doug and I set off in a five pound boat
to reminisce.
We did, about dis and dat
and dat and dis.
Though none of us spoke that way,
having impeccable diction
and sufficient distinction
to butter a five-pound loaf.
Freddy was in the dinghy;
we pulled him behind us.
He was much younger.
Though he fished and caught a five-pound flounder.
"Terribly flat," said Doug, "but what can you do?"
"Make stew," Freddy replied.
Or dis and dat. Dis:
the city Virgil and Dante
found when they got out after crossing the Styx.
"O, good, a game I can play," said Freddy, throwing
down the bundle of bright colored sticks.
Willard, Doug and I discussed how the Graf Spee
was bombed when we were eight or nine. Count Spee.
"Please make a fire," said Willard. "It's cold in the boat."
"1938." "No," I said, "1939."
"That's right," said Doug. "The Graf Spee was in a fiord."
"All aboard," said Willard,
"for World War II. Wasn't it
mysterious? We wondered what they were doing it for."
"Yes." "Yes." "Yes."

"Winken, Blinken and Nod," said Freddy.
"'By so many roots as the marsh grass sends in the sod,'"
said Willard. "I believe I have a bit of catarrh."
Freddy picked up his guitar,
"Take some honey; we've plenty of money."
Willard spooned more shad roe in his mouth,
"Do you believe he should have had to abdicate?"
"Oh, my God, no," said Doug.
"Cut off the happily-ever because
she was divorced? Dissect the princely frog?"
"Polly want a wog?" sang Freddy,
"Polly in the bog." Plink, plink.
"My mother told me," Willard said, "he wanted her
because he'd never had an orgasm before she came
slinking into his life. Isn't that mind-boggling?"
"Your mother told you?" "My mother always knew
those kinds of things," I said. "In Bergdorf Goodman,
a few months after VE day, she pointed her finger
across the floor at a sales woman dressed in blue,
'She was Eisenhower's mistress.'
And later I found out Mum was right.
Ends and means. How did they know what they knew?"
"Peas and beans." said Freddy, "Let's play."
Plink, plink. "Let's not think."
He was polite, but I could see the saw inside,
making fretwork. Soon we three
will dream beyond the blue horizon. And he will live
to fret, to clap, to sing another day.
Dat, dot, dot.

DIVINING ROD

Straight, straight as the stick which it is,
the spare rod, twiglets off, moves before
the diviner, a second prick, if you will, aroused
already before it even finds the wet, dark,
hidden place, the well-spring of desire.
We walk the field, we nonbelievers, the other
ways of finding water have been tried
and left the house site high and dry. Virgin's
Eyes are threaded through the Lover's Oracles,
and Devil's Paintbrush; they ornament the rise
we take, concealing soil which must conceal—
we hope and pray—the water for our well.

Morning light is rising, like the bread
we've left cloth-covered at the house of friends
we're staying with. The rod-man thinks dawn is
the best time for the rod to do its calisthenics.
Mercurochrome sky, as if that Christian blood—
so sanctified—had found its disinfectant.
Or is Christ buried in the earth, or sand—
I guess it was quite sandy there—unrisen?

The baby dead, and buried out in Queens
beside its great-grandmother and aunt.
And now no water. Everything is verdant
And is parched. The stick begins to twitch;
I think it is a trembling in the arm
of the diviner. And, yes, he says we will
sit down and rest. The climb has been quite steep.

The sun's sharp rim has set a bush on fire,
a thorn bush, probably *Acacia nilotica*.
Another miracle of every day.
Except when it is cloudy, or we are
in the city. O, prick-man, rod-man, angel
for the unbelievers, man disguised
as that which cannot be explained,
let's move along the lot of circumstance
and find such water as we can. For we
are near the twice-ruled boundary of our plot.

POEMS IN THIS VOLUME ARE DEDICATED AS
FOLLOWS:

Children Who Fall Off the Edge of the World:
for Scott Macdonald and Babs Noelle

What Heat Signifies:
for Glenn and Kathy Cambor

The Weekend He Died:
for Elizabeth and Frank Bernard

What No One Should Want to Have:
for Hinda and Barry Simon

The Dreamer on the Stone Couch Dreams and Wakes:
for Grace Paley

What Is Never Lost:
for Susan Wood

Casual Neglects:
for Gay Block and Malka Drucker

Who Is Chicken? AND *Retrieval:*
for E. Annie Proulx

Chicken Slippers:
for Johnny and Anne Herrmann

Once You Notice Chickens They Are Everywhere:
for Karl and Kathy Killian

Mary Cassatt's Twelve Hours in the Pleasure Quarter:
for Edward Hirsch and Janet Landay

Miriam's Grandmother and *Singing Miriam's Lament:*
for Barbara Kellerman

Maps and Globes:
for Lucia Greer

The Matter of Naming and Counting:
for Helen Frankenthaler

Leonardo's Advice to Artists:
for Jennifer Macdonald

The Great 14th Street Costume Company:
for Eve France

Dinner Before the Blue Horizon:
for Richard Howard and David Alexander

Cynthia Macdonald was born in New York City and received her B.A. from Bennington College and her M.A. from Sarah Lawrence College. She taught at Sarah Lawrence and Johns Hopkins University and is now a professor at the University of Houston, where she founded the creative writing program in 1979. Since 1972, she has published six collections of poems: *Amputations, Transplants, (W)holes, Alternate Means of Transport, Living Wills: New and Selected Poems,* and the present volume. Her grants and awards include a National Endowment for the Arts grant, a Guggenheim Fellowship, and a National Academy and Institute of Arts and Letters Award in recognition of her achievement in poetry. Formerly an opera singer, Cynthia Macdonald has written two opera librettos. She is a graduate of the Houston-Galveston Psychoanalytic Institute where she has since joined the faculty.

A NOTE ON THE TYPE

This book was set in Granjon, a computer copy of the Linotype version made by George W. Jones, who based his designs for the roman on the designs of Claude Garamond (c. 1480–1561). This Granjon more closely resembles Garamond's own work than do the various other modern types that bear his name. The *italic* of the font however *is* based on a series cut by Robert Granjon, who began his career as a type cutter in 1523 and was one of the first to practise the trade of type founder apart from that of printer.

Composition by NK Graphics, Keene, New Hampshire
Printed at The Stinehour Press, Lunenburg, Vermont
Bound at The Book Press, Brattleboro, Vermont
Typography and binding designs based on originals
by Dorothy Baker